Felix MERTIKAT | Sartep NAMIQ | Bruce STERLING | Matthias ZUBER

Temple of Refuge

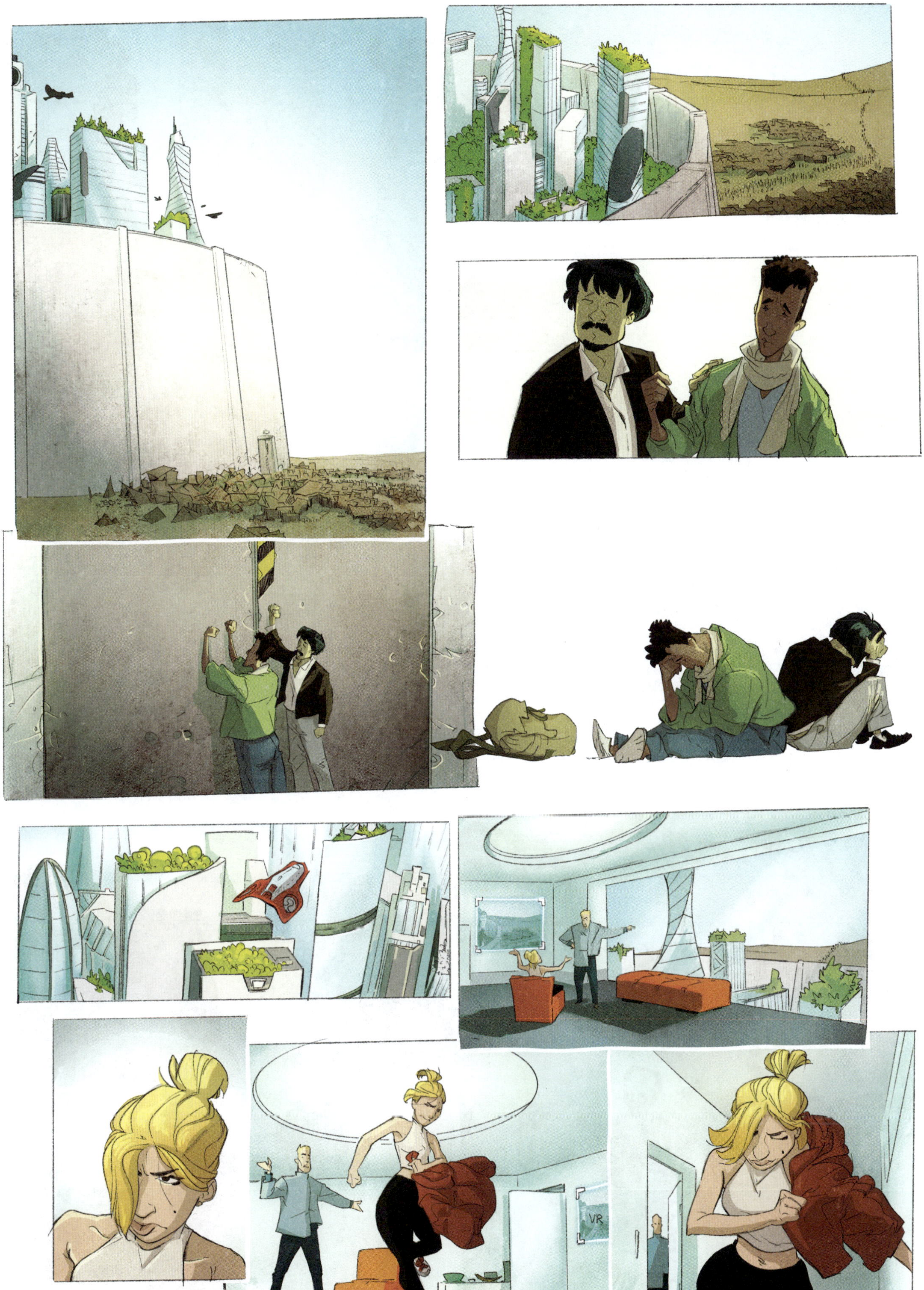
VR

101

BERLIN-TEMPELHOF

0
14:21

BVS

S

FREE TEMPELHOF
BERLIN-TEMPELHOF

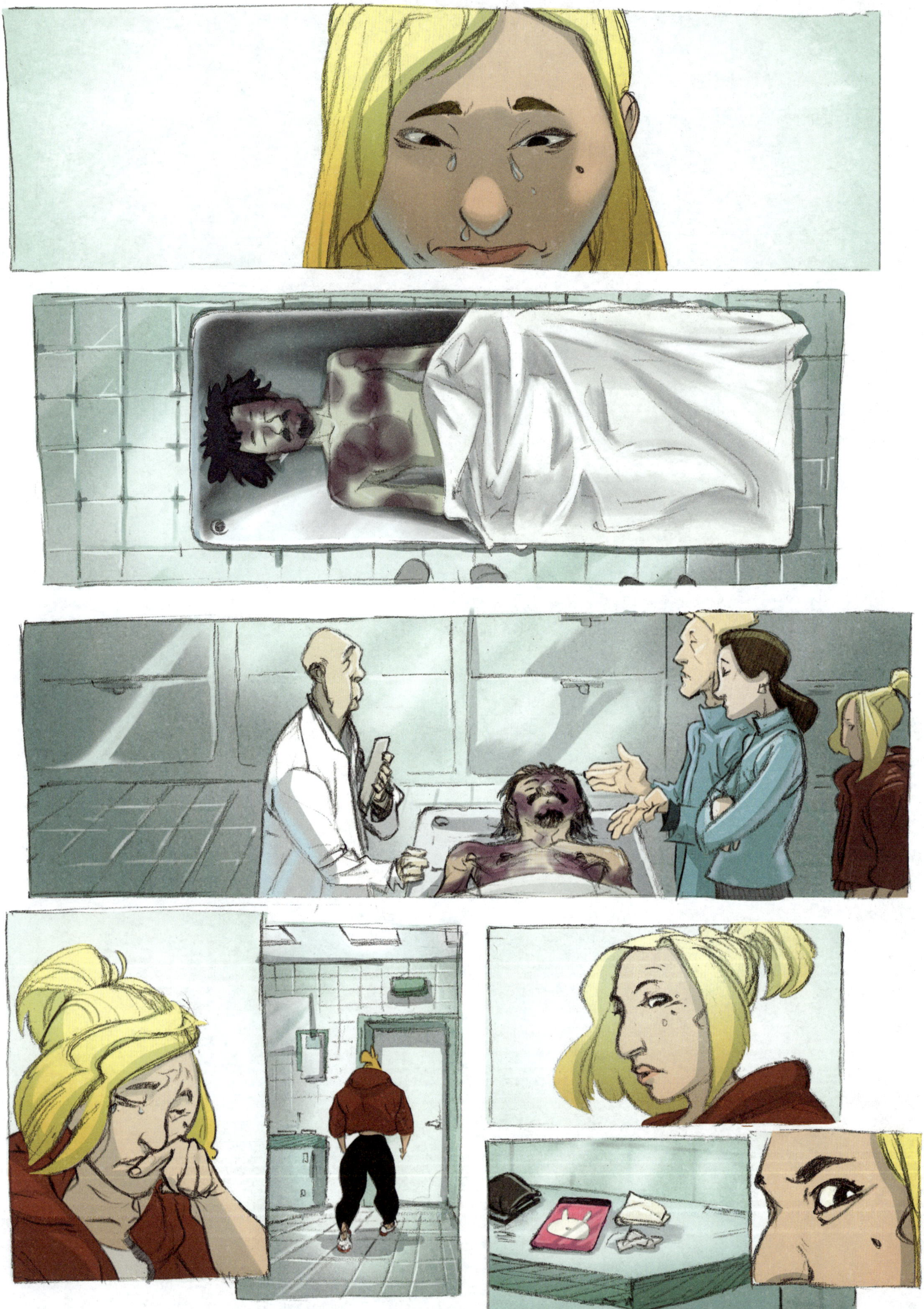

BERLIN-TEMPELHOF

E7

B7

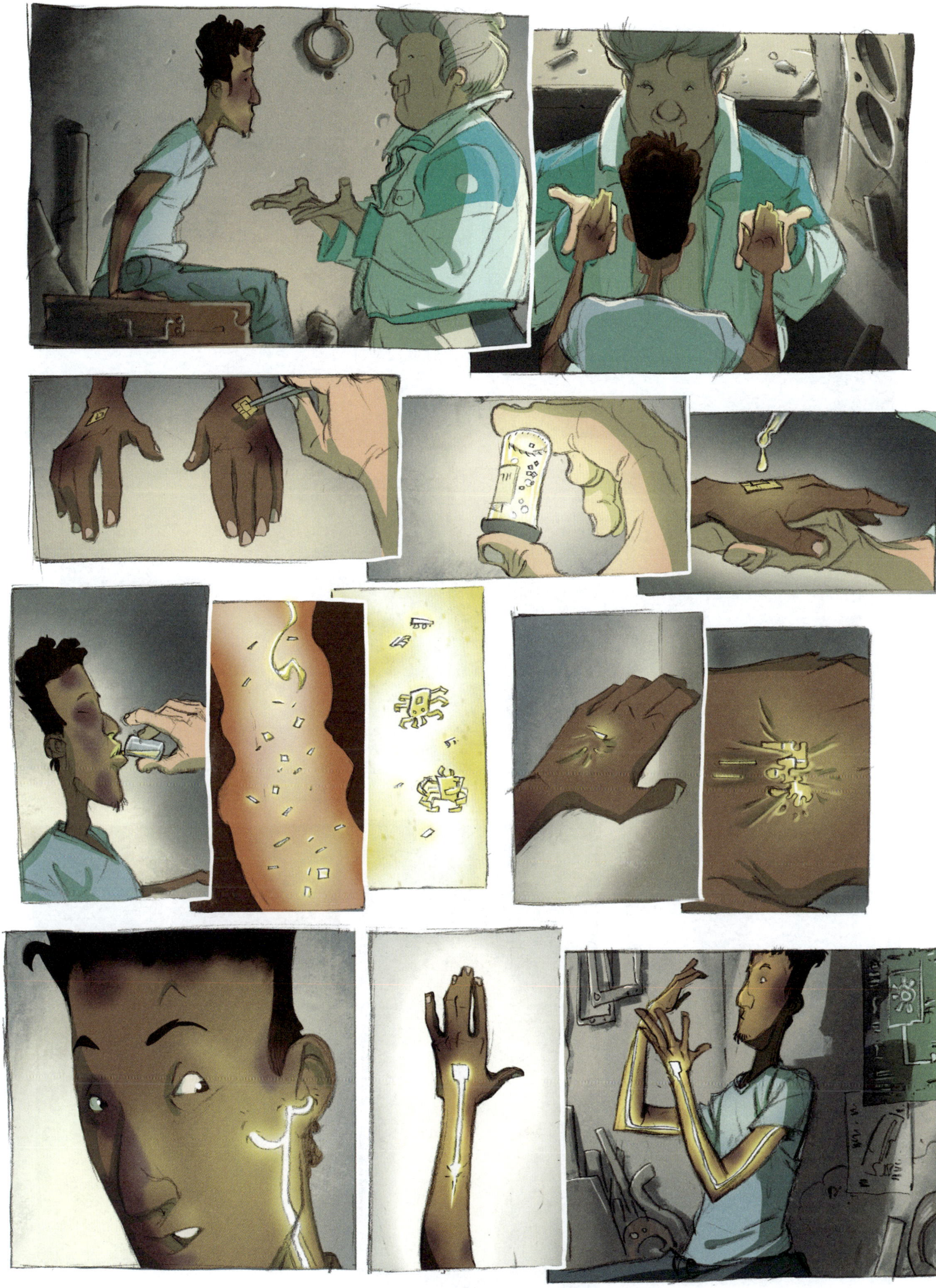

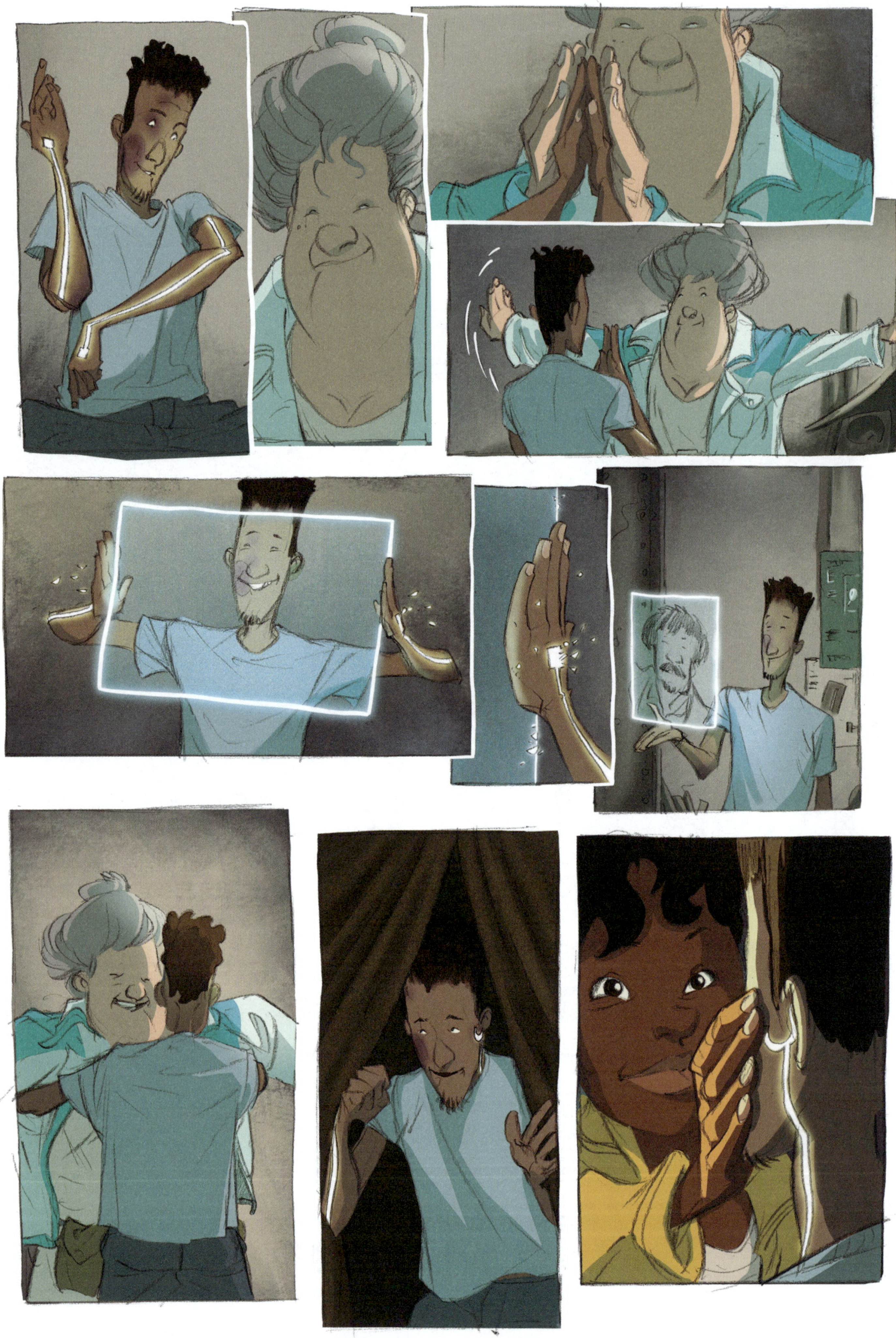

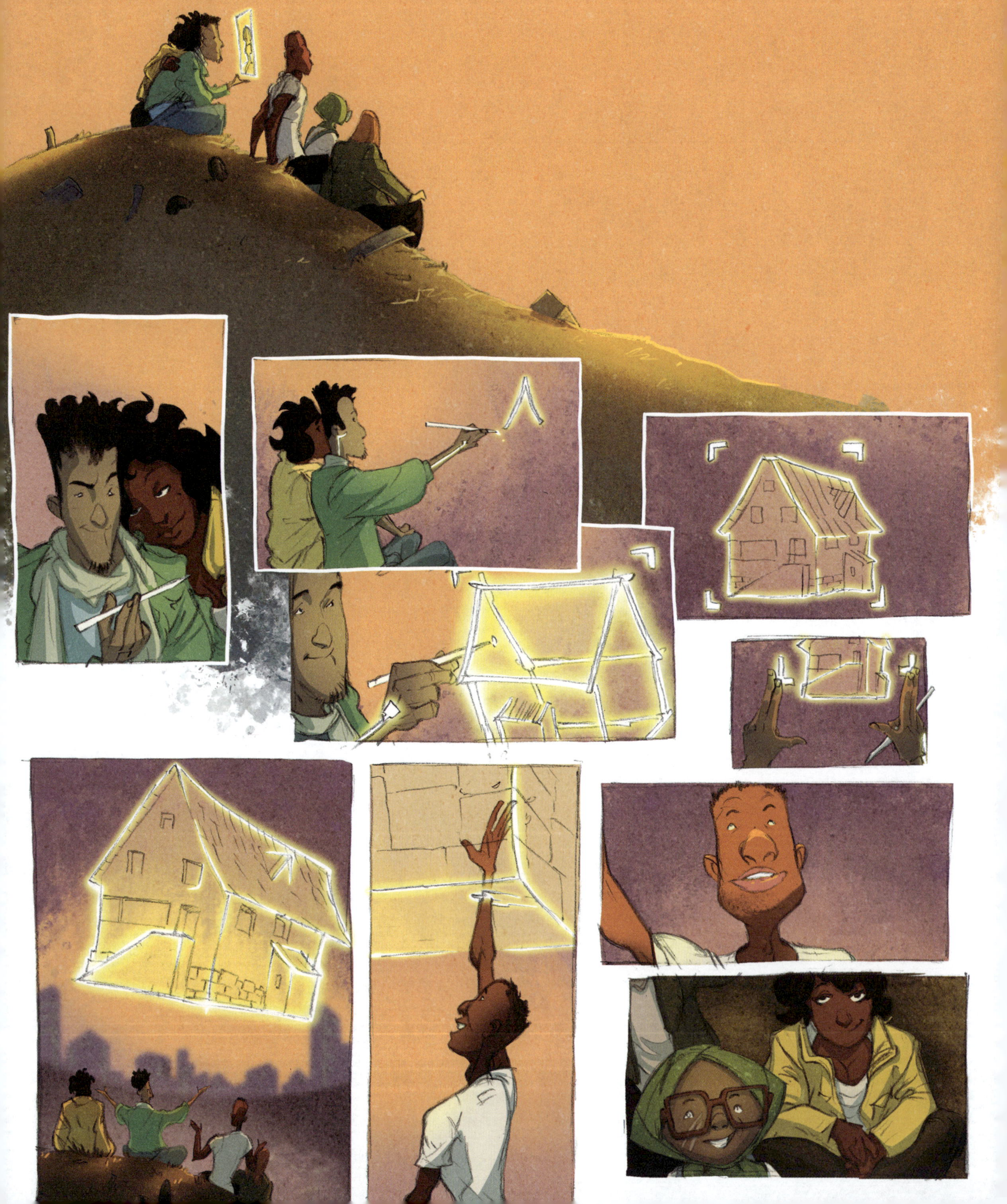

ZZZ

TEMPELHOF

164 FEET
FIELD ELEVATION
BERLIN-TEMPELHOF

Über dieses Buch

Im März 2016 kam der junge Kurde Sartep Namiq aus dem Irak nach Berlin. Er hoffte auf eine bessere Zukunft. Aber zunächst war das Leben in der Notunterkunft für geflüchtete Menschen in dem alten Flughafen Tempelhof eine Herausforderung. Zwölf Monate lang lebte er hier mit 900 anderen Menschen in einem Hangar. Wie würde es für ihn und die anderen weitergehen? Als er von dem Programm Neue Auftraggeber hörte, das Menschen dabei unterstützt, ungewöhnlich Projekte zu starten, kam ihm eine Idee: Er wollte, dass Künstler ein Comicbuch für ihn zeichnen, in dem sich die Unterkunft im Flughafen Tempelhof in eine fantastische Stadt verwandelt. Er wünschte sich eine Vision, eine Science-Fiction-Geschichte, in der alle Menschen zusammen eine bessere Welt erschaffen. Eine Welt, in der sich die Träume, die Wünsche und die Fähigkeiten aller frei entfalten können. Und so entstand dieses Buch – im Auftrag von Sartep Namiq. Viele Beteiligte haben daran mitgearbeitet, seine Idee Wirklichkeit werden zu lassen. Sie alle haben einer Bildgeschichte Leben eingehaucht, die eine schönere und bessere gemeinsame Zukunft denkbar macht – und vielleicht sogar möglich.

عن الكتاب

في آذار/ مارس عام ٢٠١٦ وصل الشاب الكردي سارتيب نامق (سەرتیپ نامیق) من العراق إلى برلين.
أمِلَ سارتيب بحياةٍ أفضل، ليواجه العيش في مركز إيواء اللاجئين المؤقت في مطار تمبلهوف، (مطار برلين الأسبق)، لمدة عام كامل، وبمشاركة ٩٠٠ لاجئ ولاجئةٍ في مهجعٍ واحد. لكن كيف للأمور أن تستمر بالنسبة إليه وللآخرين على هذا النحو؟
حينها، سمع سارتيب ببرنامج (الرعاة الجدد)، الذي يدعم الأفكار والمشاريع غير الاعتيادية.
لمعت في رأسه الفكرة، فطلب من مجموعةٍ من الفنانين رسم قصة مصورة (كوميك)، تُحوّل مكان إقامته في مطار تمبلهوف إلى مدينةٍ خيالية، حكايةٌ تحمل إطاراً ذا رؤيةٍ مستقبلية، يتعاون فيها جميع البشر لخلقِ عالمِ أفضل، عالمٌ تتحرر فيه الأحلام والأمنيات والمواهب. هكذا نشأ هذا الكتاب بتكليف من سارتيب نامق ومساهمة العديد من الأشخاص لترى فكرته النور.
معاً خلقوا قصة مصورة تطلق العنان لخيال عن مستقبل أجمل وأفضل للجميع، بل وربما أكثر من ذلك بقليل...

سەبارەت ئەم کتێبە

لە مانگی ٣ ی ساڵی ٢٠١٦، گەنجی کورد، سەرتیپ نامیق بەرەو بەرلین بەڕێکەوت لە عێراقەوە. ئەو هیوای داهاتوویەکی باشتری هەبوو. بەڵام لە سەرەتادا، ژیان لە شەڵتەرکانی فریاگووزاری بۆ پەنابەران لە فرۆکەخانەی تێمپڵۆف Tempelhof، لەگەڵ ٩٠٠ پەنابەری دیکە لە جێگایەکی تایبەت بە فرۆکەکان، بۆ ماوەی ٩ مانگ، ئاستەنگێکی گەورە بوو. ئەم بارودۆخە چۆن بەردەوام بوو بۆ ئەو و پەنابەرەکانی دیکەش؟ کاتێک سەرتیب لەبارەی پرۆگرامی نیو پاترنز New Patrons زانیاری وەرگرت کە هاوکاری خەڵک دەکات بۆ دەستپێکردنی پرۆژەکانیان، بیرۆکەیەکی هەبوو کە بریتیبوو لە کێشانی پەرتووکێکی کۆمیدی لەلایەن چەند هونەرمەندێکی وێنەکێشەوە کە گوزارشت لە ژیانی پەنابەران بکات لە چۆن جێگای نیشتەجێبوونیان لە فڕۆکەخانەی تێمپڵۆف Tempelhof گۆڕیوە بۆ شارێکی ناوازە. ئەو خەونێکی هەبوو، چیرۆکێکی زانستی خەیاڵی کە تیایدا مرۆڤەکان پێکەوە جیهانێکی باشتر بنیاتبنێن. جیهانێک کە خەون و ئاوات و تواناکانمان بە ئازادی گەشەبکەن. بەم جۆرە ئەم پەرتوکە نوسرا و بەرهەمهێنرا لەلایەن سەرتیپ نامیق. کەسانێکی زۆر لە بەدیهێنانی ئەم بیرۆکەیە بەشداربوون. هەموویان بەشداربوون لە ژیانبەخشین لە وێنە چیرۆکیەکان کە داهاتوویەکی جوانتر و باشتر پێکەوە بنیاتدەنێت.

About this book

In March 2016 a young Kurd, Sartep Namiq, came to Berlin from Iraq, hoping for a better future. His first 12 months in the city were a challenge, living in the emergency shelter for refugees with 900 others in a hangar in the former Tempelhof airport. How would things work out for him and those around him? Then Sartep heard of the New Patrons program, which supports people in creating unusual projects, and he had an idea! Sartep's concept was to have artists transform the refugee accommodation at Tempelhof Airport into a fantastical city, through an original comic book. He envisioned a tale of science fiction, that encapsulates the need of the residents to create a better world for themselves, one in which their dreams and wishes unfold freely and their skills and abilities are put to good use. Many have collaborated to make this idea into a reality, each breathing life into an illustrated story, that makes a better, more beautiful future together conceivable – and maybe even possible.

Kitap Hakkında

Mart 2016'da bir kürt genci Sartep Namiq, Irak'tan Berlin'e geldi. Daha iyi bir geleceğin hayalini kuruyordu. Ancak başlangıçta, on iki ay boyunca 900 kişiyle birlikte eski Tempelhof Havaalanı hangarındaki geçiçi mülteci barınağında yaşamak, bir mücadeleydi. O ve diğerleri için hayat nasıl devam edebilirdi? İnsanları bu konuda destekleyen sıradışı Neue Auftraggeber Programının başladığını duyduğunda aklına bir fikir geldi. Sanatçılardan, onun için Tempelhof Havaalanı'nda bulunan mülteci barınağının fantastik bir şehir olarak anlatıldığı bir çizgi roman çizmesini istedi. Daha iyi bir dünya yaratmak için tüm insanların birlikte çalışabileceği bir düş, bir bilim kurgu hikayesi istiyordu. Herkesin düşlerini, dileklerini, yeteneklerini özgürce sergileyebileceği bir dünya. Ve böylece bu kitap Sartep Namiq adına ortaya çıktı. Birçok katılımcı Sartep Namiq'in fikrini gerçekleştirmek için birlikte çalıştı. Hepsi birlikte daha güzel ve daha iyi bir gelecek düşüne resimli bir hikayeyle hayat verdiler, hatta aslında biraz daha mümkün kıldılar.

Об этой книге

В марте 2016 года молодой курд Сартеп Намик приехал в Берлин из Ирака. Он надеялся на лучшее будущее. Поначалу жизнь в лагере для беженцев в старом аэропорту Темпельхоф была совсем непростой. Двенадцать месяцев он жил в ангаре, где были размещены 900 человек. Что ждет его впереди, как сложится жизнь у остальных? Когда он услышал о программе „Новые заказчики“, цель которой поддерживать необычные проекты, у него возникла идея: а что если художники нарисуют комикс, в котором лагерь для беженцев в аэропорту Темпельхоф превратится в фантастический город. Ему представлялся рассказ в картинках в жанре научной фантастики, история, в которой люди все вместе создают лучший мир, в котором мечты и желания воплощаются в жизнь и в котором каждый может свободно развиваться. И так по заказу Сартепа Намика появилась эта книга. Многие были вовлечены в творческий процесс, работали вместе, чтобы воплотить его идею в жизнь. Художники оживили эту историю и создали образ нашего совместного будущего, лучшего и вполне возможного, и сделали его тем самым пусть немного, но более возможным.

À propos de ce livre

En mars 2016, le jeune Kurde Sartep Namiq est arrivé à Berlin en provenance d‘Irak. Pendant douze mois, il s’est retrouvé à devoir vivre avec 900 autres personnes dans un hangar de l‘ancien aéroport de Tempelhof dans lequel avait été construit des abris d’urgence. Comment, dans cette situation, imaginer l’avenir, pour lui et pour les autres ? Lorsqu‘il a entendu parler du programme Nouveaux Commanditaires, qui aide les gens à prendre l’initiative et lancer des projets de création, une idée lui est venue : il voulait que des artistes lui dessinent une bande dessinée dans laquelle le logement des réfugiés à l‘aéroport de Tempelhof deviendrait une ville fantastique. Il voulait une vision, une histoire de science-fiction dans laquelle tous les gens créent ensemble un monde dans lequel les rêves, les souhaits et les capacités de chacun peuvent s‘épanouir librement. C‘est ainsi qu‘a été réalisé ce livre commandé par Sartep Namiq. De nombreuses personnes se sont impliquées pour faire de son idée une réalité et insuffler la vie à une histoire qui grâce aux images rend concevable la possibilité d’un avenir meilleur.

Impressum / Imprint / الناشرون / چاپ کردن / Выходные данные / Baskı / Impressum

Im Auftrag von / Commissioned by / تكليف / لەلایەن / По заказу / Talebi üzerine / Commandé par: Sartep Namiq
Geschichte / Story / قصة / چیرۆک / История / Hikaye / Récit: Christopher Tauber, Matthias Zuber
Nach einer Idee von / Based on an idea by / فكرة / بنەمای بیرۆکە لەلایەن / Идея / Fikir / Basé sur une idée de: Bruce Sterling
Illustration / Illustration / رسوم / نەخشەکردن / Иллюстрации / İllüstrasyon / Illustration: Felix Mertikat
Farbe / Colors / الألوان / ڕەنگەکان / Цвет / Renkler / Couleurs: Jacob Müller

Mediation und Leitung / Mediation and direction / إدارة ووساطة / نێوەندو ئاراستە / Медиатор и руководитель / Kolaylaştırma ve Yönetim / Médiation et direction: Alexander Koch
Ko-Mediation / Co-mediation / الوسطاء المشاركون / هاو-نێوەند / Ко-медиация / Eş Kolaylaştırıcı / Co-médiation: Natasha Aruri, Soran Ahmet
Projektleitung / Project management / إدارة المشروع / بەڕێوەبردنی پرۆژە / Руководители проекта / Proje Yönetimi / Gestion de projet: Julia Jung, Karola Matschke, Franziska Benger
Pressearbeit / Press relations / علاقات عامة / پەیوەندی ڕۆژنامەوانی / Работа со СМИ / Basınla İlişkiler / Relations de presse: Denhart von Harling
Team / Team / أسرة العمل / ستافی / Команда / Takım / Équipe Die Gesellschaft der Neuen Auftraggeber: Boushra Adi, Kathrin Aichele, Anna Freedman, Stefanie Kinsky, David Magnus, Henriette Sölter

Vielen Dank für die Unterstützung / Thanks for collaboration and support / شكر خاص لكل من ساهم في انجاز ودعم هذا العمل / سوپاس بۆ هاوکاری و پشتیوانی / Благодарность за поддержку / Destekleri için teşekkürler / Merci pour le soutien apporté: Eyas Adi, Nika Dubrovsky, Hiwa K, Khaled Al Masri, Jasmin Mertikat, Razwan Anwar Mohamad, François Schuiten, Ayaz Shalal Kado, Wolf Stegmaier and Team Egmont Comic Collection, Tamaja GmbH, Jasmina Tesanovic, Team Federal Foreign Office (Andreas Görgen, Hana Becker, Sarah Duryea, Thomas Friebel, Julia Harrer, Katrin Ramirez Viveros, Petra Reineke-Lagarde, Christian Nell), Team Institute for Foreign Cultural Relations (Ev Fischer, Jochen Hetterich, Elke aus dem Moore, Annika Niemann, Alya Sebti, Tanja Spiess)

NEUE AUFTRAGGEBER www.neueauftraggeber.de

In Kooperation mit / In collaboration with / بالتعاون مع / به هاوبەشی لەگەڵ / Совместно с / İşbirliğiyle / En collaboration avec:

ifa Institut für Auslandsbeziehungen

Gefördert von / Funded by / بتمويل من / پشتگیری دارایی له لایەن / При финансовой поддержке / Fon verenler / Soutenu par:

Auswärtiges Amt

Unterstützt von / Supported by / بدعم من / پشتیوانی کراوه لەلایەن / При поддержке / Destekçiler / Avec l'aide de:

Fondation de France

Ein Menschenleben ist unbezahlbar, Seenotrettung ist es nicht.
Der Erlös des Buches geht direkt und in vollem Umfang an

Sea-Watch.org

Weitere Informationen unter https://sea-watch.org/

www.temple-of-refuge.net